# THE GRATITUDE JOURNAL

By Fitrah Designs

# GRATITUDE

Is a feeling of appreciation and being thankful for the good things that happen in your life. Research suggests that centralising experiences through writing in a gratitude journal is spiritually therapeutic, reduces stress, increases happiness, and improves self-esteem. Recording and transcribing our thoughts grants us an intimate insight into ourselves and allows us to translate appreciation from our thoughts to reality.

This journal is designed to help you truly savour what you appreciate as it prompts you to write what makes you happy. A tip is to go for depth rather than breadth as just writing down a list of nice thoughts will soon become monotonous. Writing about what truly makes you happy from the simple things to the greater things in life will allow you to have a new sense of appreciation for every gift you possess.

It's ok if you can't write every day — write when you feel inspired too and don't sweat the grammar and spelling. No one will see this journal unless you want them to. Don't think of this journal as a self-improvement project but an opportunity to allow your thoughts to come to life. An area just for you to reflect on the above and beyond things that make you grateful.

# EXAMPLE GUIDE

Here are some journaling prompts
(Note: The use of prompts is optional):
Feel free to write about anything for which you are grateful.

*Something beautiful I saw...*
*The best part about today...*
*Something I can be proud of...*
*A fun experience I had...*
*A valuable lesson I've learnt...*
*An unexpected good thing that happened...*
*An act of kindness I witnessed or received...*

## What is my mood today?

*I am happy today as I have my awesome gratitude journal to fill and help me keep a balanced mental attitude.*

**Date:** 19th October

## What am I grateful for?

I'm grateful for all the people that were involved in the making of this gratitude journal. I'm especially grateful for my thoughts. I have a lot of them (a lot, a lot!) and I'm thankful for every single one.

The thought of a gratitude journal has finally come to life and I'm thankful for the people that have supported and encouraged me to get this project done. I can't help but smile as I read the quotes and see the funny faces in this journal. I am also thankful for the concept of the journal as it will hopefully allow me to keep a positive outlook on my thoughts and surroundings.

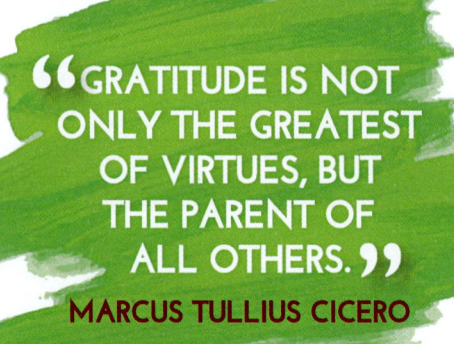

> **GRATITUDE IS NOT ONLY THE GREATEST OF VIRTUES, BUT THE PARENT OF ALL OTHERS.**
>
> **MARCUS TULLIUS CICERO**

## What is my mood today?

_____
_____
_____
_____
_____
_____
_____

# Date

## What am I grateful for?

> **I WOULD MAINTAIN THAT THANKS ARE THE HIGHEST FORM OF THOUGHT, AND THAT GRATITUDE IS HAPPINESS DOUBLED BY WONDER.**
>
> G.K. CHESTERTON

## What is my mood today?

# Date

## What am I grateful for?

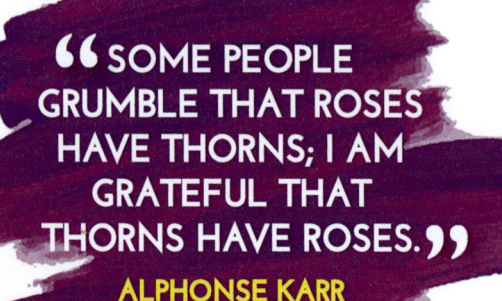

> **"SOME PEOPLE GRUMBLE THAT ROSES HAVE THORNS; I AM GRATEFUL THAT THORNS HAVE ROSES."**
> — ALPHONSE KARR

## What is my mood today?

_____
_____
_____
_____
_____
_____
_____

# Date

## What am I grateful for?

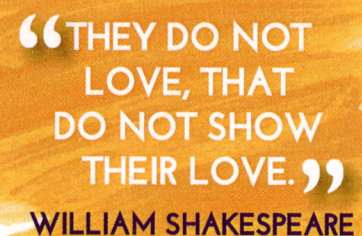

> **"THEY DO NOT LOVE, THAT DO NOT SHOW THEIR LOVE."**
> **WILLIAM SHAKESPEARE**

## What is my mood today?

_____
_____
_____
_____
_____
_____
_____

**Date** ..................................................

## What am I grateful for?

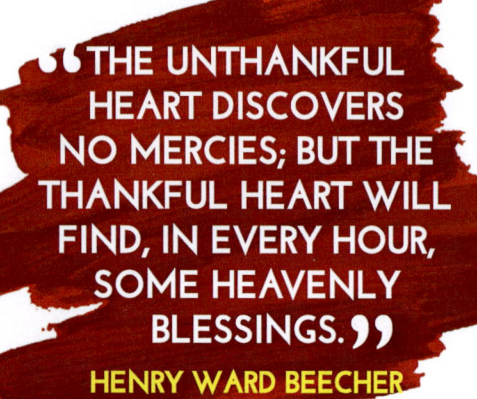

> **"THE UNTHANKFUL HEART DISCOVERS NO MERCIES; BUT THE THANKFUL HEART WILL FIND, IN EVERY HOUR, SOME HEAVENLY BLESSINGS."**
>
> **HENRY WARD BEECHER**

## What is my mood today?

_____
_____
_____
_____
_____
_____
_____

# Date

## What am I grateful for?

> **"HE IS A WISE MAN WHO DOES NOT GRIEVE FOR THE THINGS WHICH HE HAS NOT, BUT REJOICES FOR THOSE WHICH HE HAS."**
>
> **EPICTETUS**

## What is my mood today?

_____
_____
_____
_____
_____
_____
_____

# Date

## What am I grateful for?

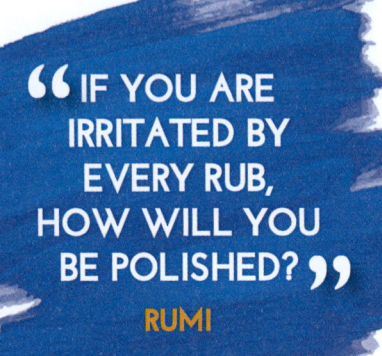

> **"IF YOU ARE IRRITATED BY EVERY RUB, HOW WILL YOU BE POLISHED?"**
>
> **RUMI**

## What is my mood today?

_____
_____
_____
_____
_____
_____
_____

# Date

## What am I grateful for?

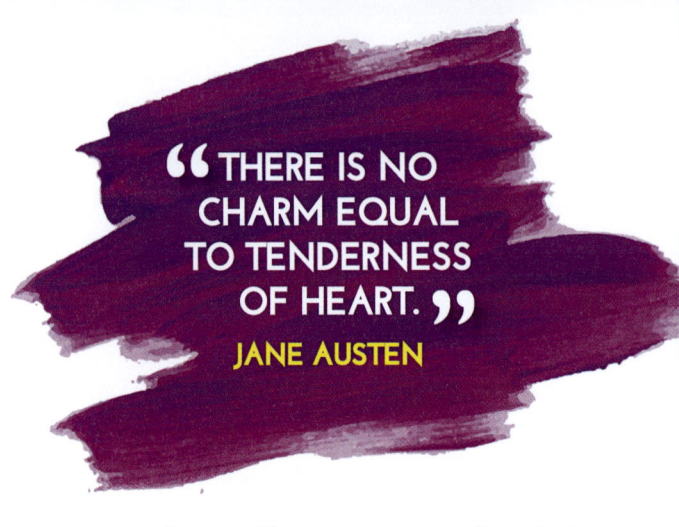

> **THERE IS NO CHARM EQUAL TO TENDERNESS OF HEART.**
> — JANE AUSTEN

### What is my mood today?

_____
_____
_____
_____
_____
_____
_____
_____

# Date

## What am I grateful for?

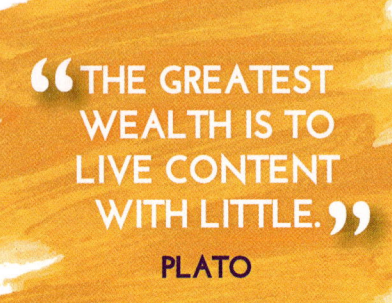

> **THE GREATEST WEALTH IS TO LIVE CONTENT WITH LITTLE.**
>
> **PLATO**

## What is my mood today?

_____
_____
_____
_____
_____
_____
_____
_____

Date ...................................................

## What am I grateful for?

_____
_____
_____
_____
_____
_____
_____
_____
_____
_____
_____
_____
_____
_____
_____
_____
_____
_____
_____
_____

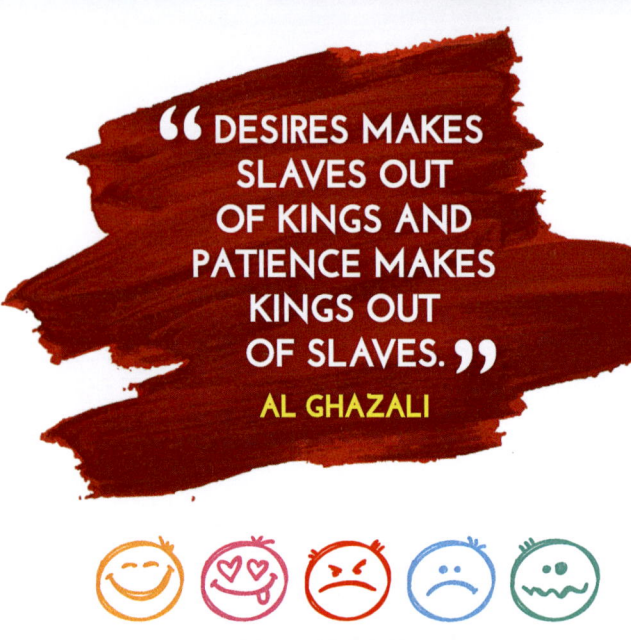

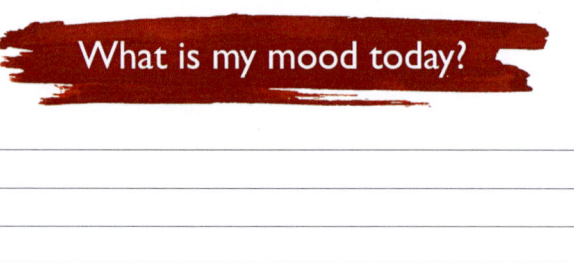

> **DESIRES MAKES SLAVES OUT OF KINGS AND PATIENCE MAKES KINGS OUT OF SLAVES.**
>
> **AL GHAZALI**

## What is my mood today?

_____
_____
_____
_____
_____
_____
_____

**Date** ..............................................

## What am I grateful for?

_____
_____
_____
_____
_____
_____
_____
_____
_____
_____
_____
_____
_____
_____
_____
_____
_____
_____
_____

> **SHOWING GRATITUDE WILL GIVE YOU THINGS TO BE THANKFUL ABOUT AND SHOWING INGRATITUDE WILL GIVE YOU THINGS TO COMPLAIN ABOUT.**
>
> UNKNOWN

## What is my mood today?

___
___
___
___
___
___
___

## Date

## What am I grateful for?

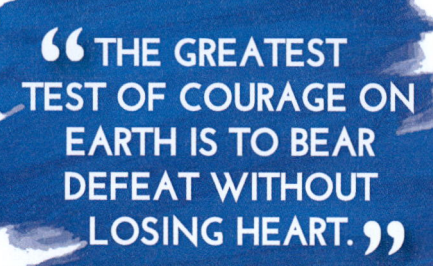

> **THE GREATEST TEST OF COURAGE ON EARTH IS TO BEAR DEFEAT WITHOUT LOSING HEART.**
>
> ROBERT GREEN INGERSOLL

## What is my mood today?

_____
_____
_____
_____
_____
_____
_____

# Date

## What am I grateful for?

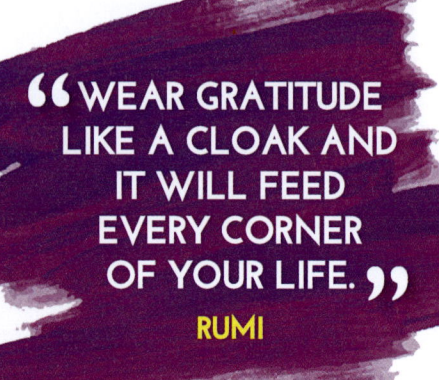

> **WEAR GRATITUDE LIKE A CLOAK AND IT WILL FEED EVERY CORNER OF YOUR LIFE.**
>
> **RUMI**

## What is my mood today?

_____
_____
_____
_____
_____
_____
_____

# Date

## What am I grateful for?

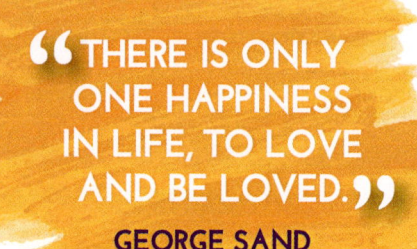

> **"THERE IS ONLY ONE HAPPINESS IN LIFE, TO LOVE AND BE LOVED."**
> **GEORGE SAND**

## What is my mood today?

_____
_____
_____
_____
_____
_____
_____

**Date** ..................................................

## What am I grateful for?

_____
_____
_____
_____
_____
_____
_____
_____
_____
_____
_____
_____
_____
_____
_____
_____
_____
_____
_____

> **"WHEN YOU ARISE IN THE MORNING, THINK OF WHAT A PRECIOUS PRIVILEGE IT IS TO BE ALIVE – TO BREATHE, TO THINK, TO ENJOY, TO LOVE."**
>
> **MARCUS AURELIUS**

### What is my mood today?

_____
_____
_____
_____
_____
_____
_____

# Date

## What am I grateful for?

> **"WE ALWAYS TAKE CREDIT FOR THE GOOD, AND ATTRIBUTE THE BAD TO FORTUNE."**
> **LA FONTAINE**

## What is my mood today?

_____
_____
_____
_____
_____
_____
_____
_____

# Date

## What am I grateful for?

> "HAPPINESS IS THE ONLY GOOD. THE TIME TO BE HAPPY IS NOW. THE PLACE TO BE HAPPY IS HERE. THE WAY TO BE HAPPY IS TO MAKE OTHERS SO."
>
> ROBERT GREEN INGERSOLL

## What is my mood today?

_____
_____
_____
_____
_____
_____
_____

# Date

## What am I grateful for?

> **"TO GET WHAT YOU LOVE, YOU MUST FIRST BE PATIENT WITH WHAT YOU HATE."**
>
> — AL-GHAZALI

## What is my mood today?

_____
_____
_____
_____
_____
_____
_____

# Date

## What am I grateful for?

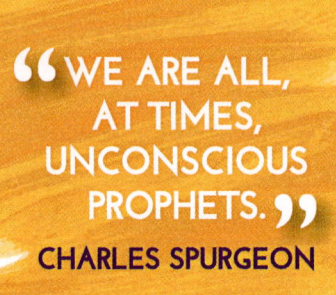

> "WE ARE ALL, AT TIMES, UNCONSCIOUS PROPHETS."
> **CHARLES SPURGEON**

## What is my mood today?

_____
_____
_____
_____
_____
_____
_____

Date ..................................................

## What am I grateful for?

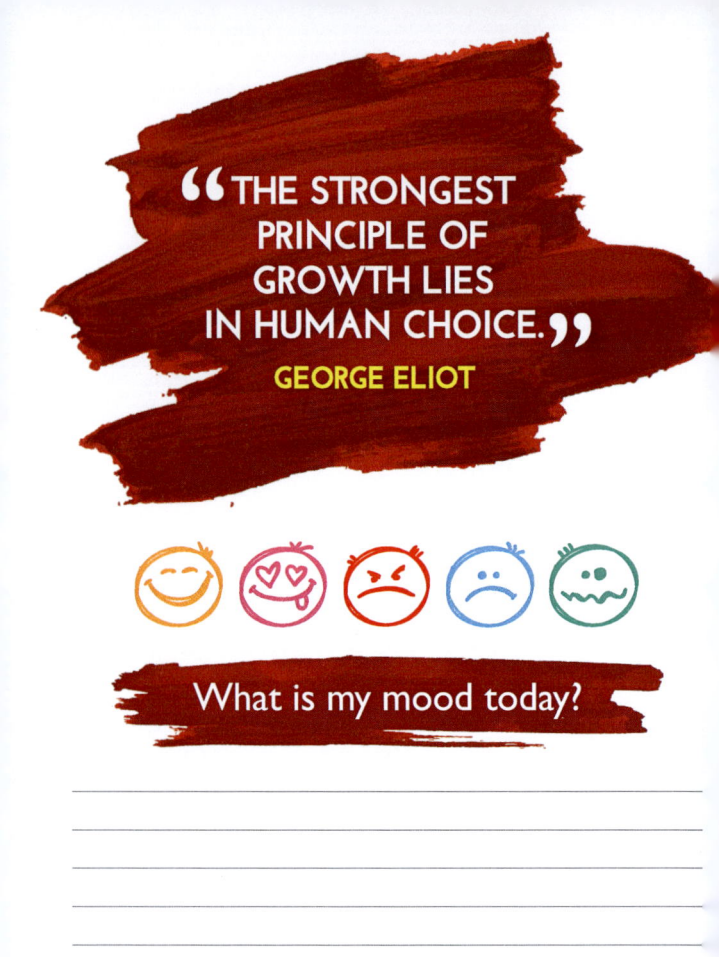

> **"THE STRONGEST PRINCIPLE OF GROWTH LIES IN HUMAN CHOICE."**
> — GEORGE ELIOT

## What is my mood today?

_____
_____
_____
_____
_____
_____
_____

**Date** ..................................................

## What am I grateful for?

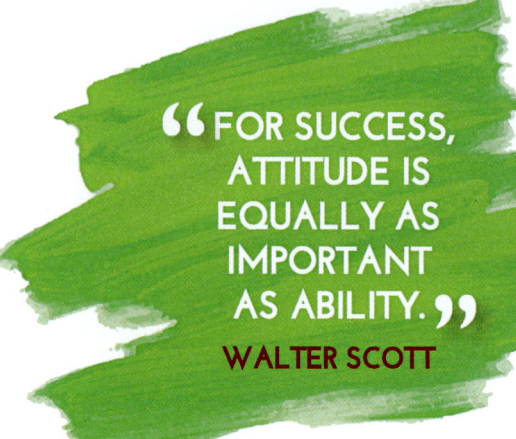

> **FOR SUCCESS, ATTITUDE IS EQUALLY AS IMPORTANT AS ABILITY.**
>
> **WALTER SCOTT**

## What is my mood today?

_____
_____
_____
_____
_____
_____
_____

# Date

## What am I grateful for?

> **ONE DAY OR DAY ONE. YOU DECIDE.**
>
> UNKNOWN

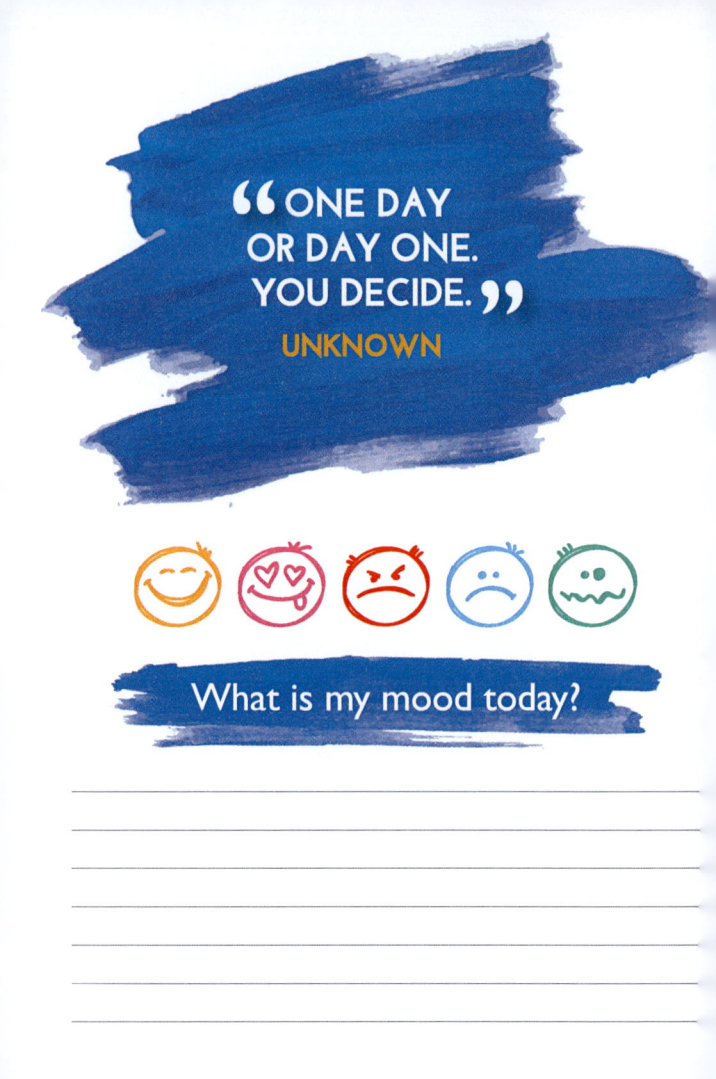

## What is my mood today?

_____
_____
_____
_____
_____
_____
_____
_____

# Date

## What am I grateful for?

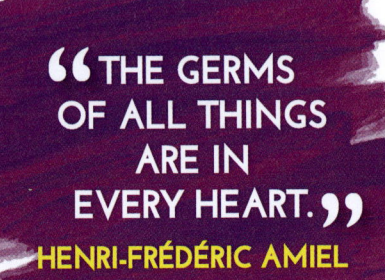

> **"THE GERMS OF ALL THINGS ARE IN EVERY HEART."**
>
> **HENRI-FRÉDÉRIC AMIEL**

## What is my mood today?

_____
_____
_____
_____
_____
_____
_____
_____

# Date

## What am I grateful for?

> **INHALE INSPIRATION, EXHALE TALENT.**
>
> UNKNOWN

## What is my mood today?

_____
_____
_____
_____
_____
_____
_____
_____

Date ..............................................

## What am I grateful for?

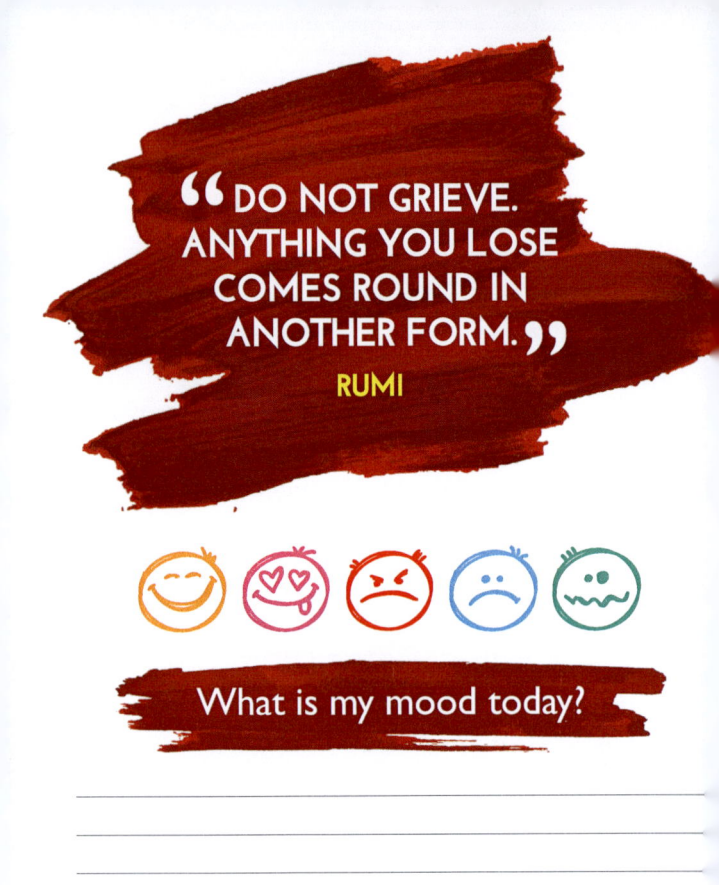

> **DO NOT GRIEVE. ANYTHING YOU LOSE COMES ROUND IN ANOTHER FORM.**
>
> **RUMI**

## What is my mood today?

_____
_____
_____
_____
_____
_____
_____
_____

**Date** ..........................................

## What am I grateful for?

> **LIBERTY NOT LIBERTINE.**
>
> **SHABBIR MELLICK**

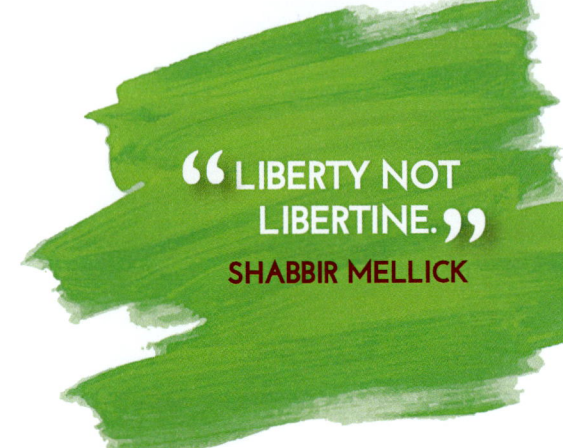

## What is my mood today?

_____
_____
_____
_____
_____
_____
_____

## Date

## What am I grateful for?